T0387379

**Greetings, brown bears!**

1

MARVELS ANIMALS 19

# BROWN BEARS

QUINN M. ARNOLD

CREATIVE EDUCATION | CREATIVE PAPERBACKS

# table of contents

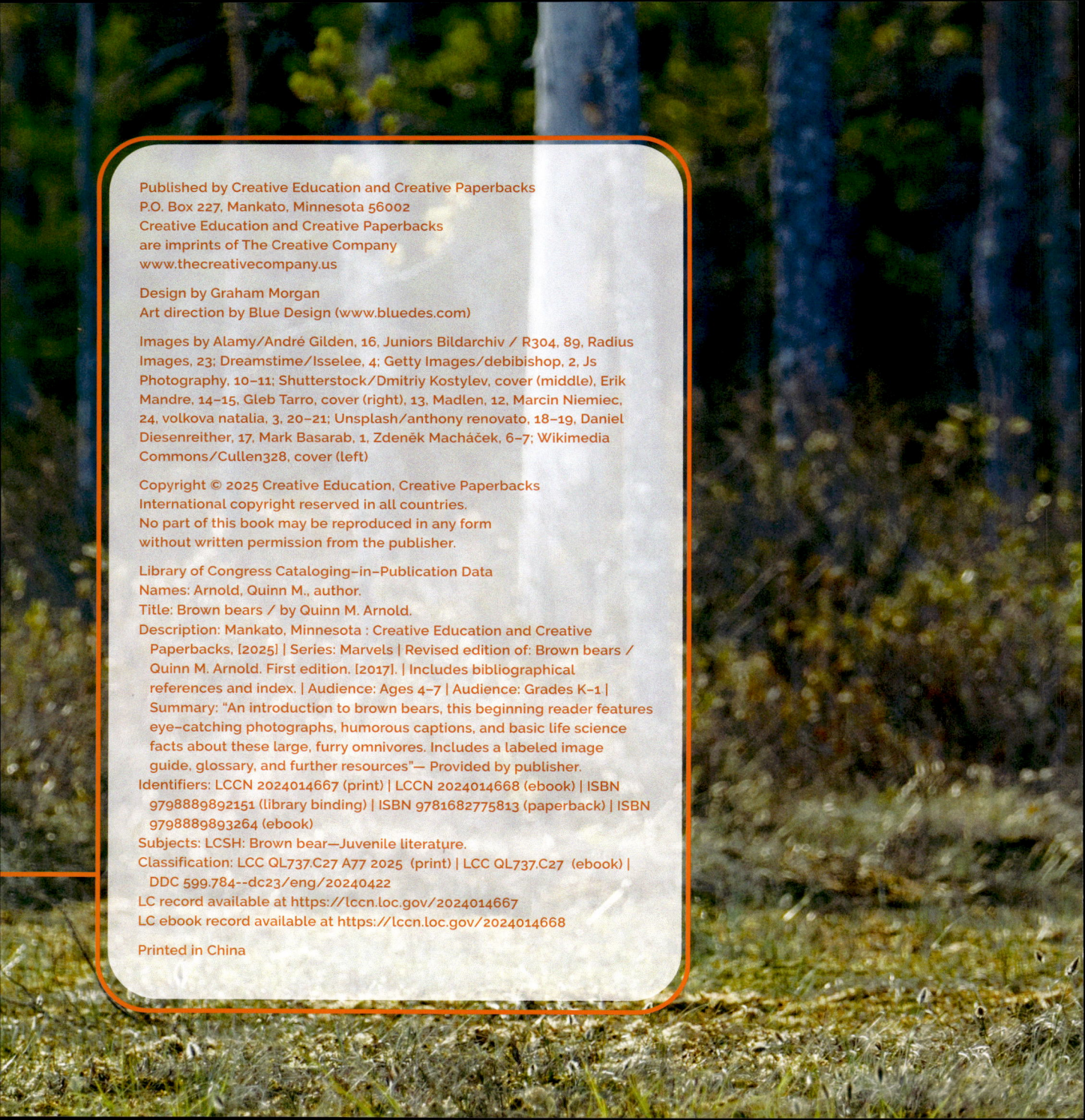

Published by Creative Education and Creative Paperbacks
P.O. Box 227, Mankato, Minnesota 56002
Creative Education and Creative Paperbacks
are imprints of The Creative Company
www.thecreativecompany.us

Design by Graham Morgan
Art direction by Blue Design (www.bluedes.com)

Images by Alamy/André Gilden, 16, Juniors Bildarchiv / R304, 89, Radius Images, 23; Dreamstime/Isselee, 4; Getty Images/debibishop, 2, Js Photography, 10–11; Shutterstock/Dmitriy Kostylev, cover (middle), Erik Mandre, 14–15, Gleb Tarro, cover (right), 13, Madlen, 12, Marcin Niemiec, 24, volkova natalia, 3, 20–21; Unsplash/anthony renovato, 18–19, Daniel Diesenreither, 17, Mark Basarab, 1, Zdeněk Macháček, 6–7; Wikimedia Commons/Cullen328, cover (left)

Library of Congress Cataloging–in–Publication Data
Names: Arnold, Quinn M., author.
Title: Brown bears / by Quinn M. Arnold.
Description: Mankato, Minnesota : Creative Education and Creative Paperbacks, [2025] | Series: Marvels | Revised edition of: Brown bears / Quinn M. Arnold. First edition. [2017]. | Includes bibliographical references and index. | Audience: Ages 4–7 | Audience: Grades K–1 | Summary: "An introduction to brown bears, this beginning reader features eye–catching photographs, humorous captions, and basic life science facts about these large, furry omnivores. Includes a labeled image guide, glossary, and further resources"— Provided by publisher.
Identifiers: LCCN 2024014667 (print) | LCCN 2024014668 (ebook) | ISBN 9798889892151 (library binding) | ISBN 9781682775813 (paperback) | ISBN 9798889893264 (ebook)
Subjects: LCSH: Brown bear—Juvenile literature.
Classification: LCC QL737.C27 A77 2025  (print) | LCC QL737.C27  (ebook) | DDC 599.784--dc23/eng/20240422
LC record available at https://lccn.loc.gov/2024014667
LC ebook record available at https://lccn.loc.gov/2024014668

Printed in China

Brown bears are big. Their strong shoulders make a hump. Many brown bears live in forests.

Big brown bears have thick **fur**. It can be light brown to black. It keeps them warm when they **hibernate**.

9

Brown bears can remember a lot. They know where to find **dens**. They know where to find food.

11

Bears eat a lot of plants and grass. They eat meat, too. Brown bears catch fish with their sharp teeth and claws.

TIME FOR DESSERT!

MOM'S FAVORITE

14

Bear babies are called cubs. Cubs climb up trees. They live with their mother.

**Brown bears sniff the air. They catch fish in the river.**

17

# [ Picture a Brown Bear ]

FUR

LEG

PAW

20

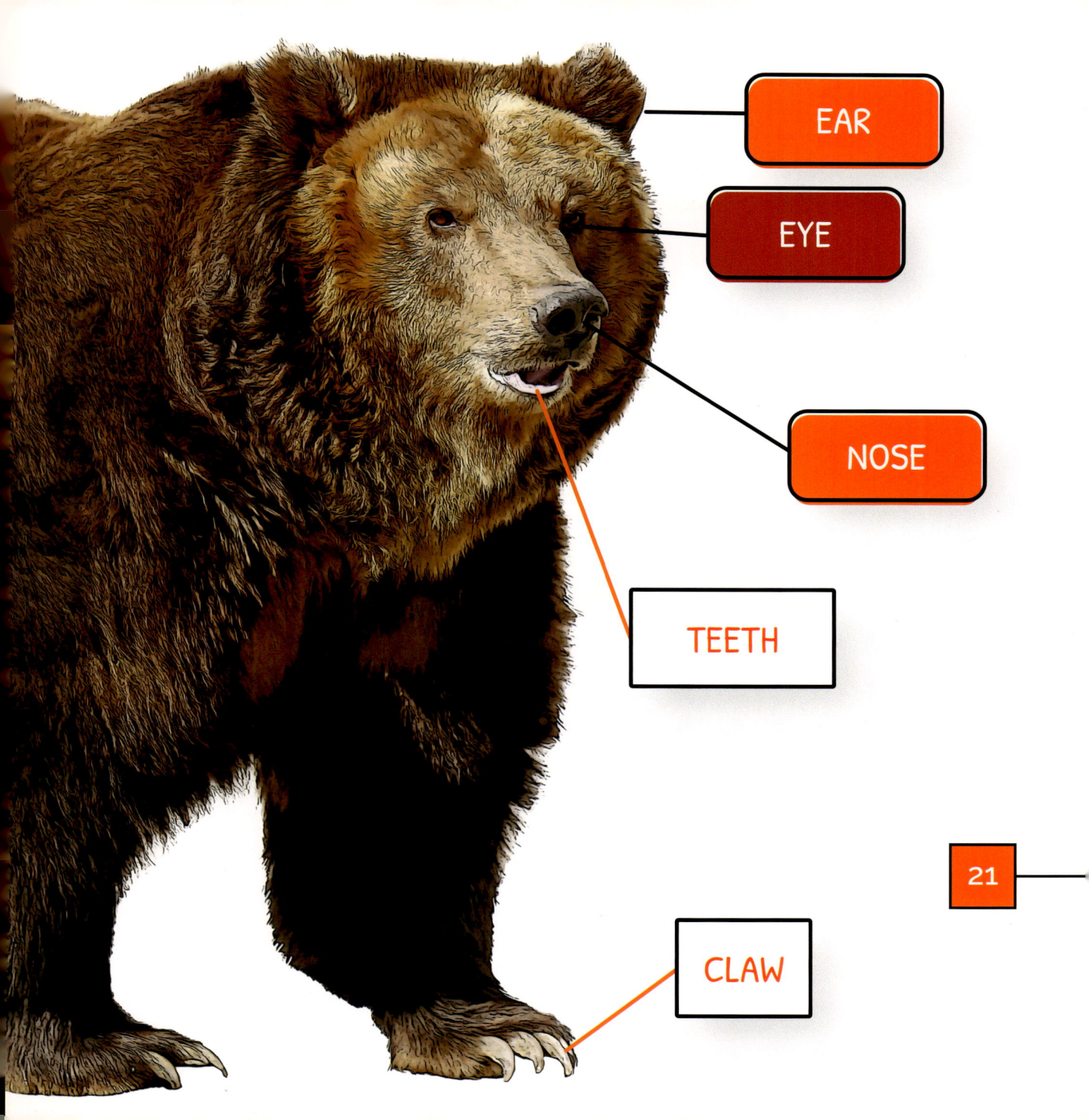

EAR

EYE

NOSE

TEETH

21

CLAW

## WORDS TO KNOW

**den:** an enclosed space, such as a cave, where bears hibernate

**fur:** the short, hairy coat of an animal

**hibernate:** to spend the winter sleeping

## READ MORE

Crumpton, Nick. *Brown Bears*. Somerville, Mass.: Candlewick Press, 2024.

Riggs, Kate. *Brown Bears*. Mankato, Minn.: The Creative Company, 2023.

## WEBSITES

Brown Bear
https://sdzwildlifeexplorers.org/animals/brown-bear

Learn about brown bears from the San Diego Zoo.

National Geographic Kids: Brown Bear
https://kids.nationalgeographic.com/animals/mammals/facts/brown-bear

Discover more about the brown bear and how it lives.

23

## INDEX